All About
THAILAND

Stories, Songs, Crafts and Games for Kids

ELAINE RUSSELL

Illustrated by

PATCHAREE MEESUKHON & VINIT YEESMAN

TUTTLE Publishing

Tokyo | Rutland, Vermont | Singapore

Contents

Hello – Sawatdi Kha
(Sa-wat-de Ka)

This is how to say "hello" in Thailand if you are a girl. Boys say *sawatdi khrap* (sa-wat-de kra). When we meet, we make a *wai* by bowing our head and putting our hands together under our chins as a sign of respect.

Mali

My name is Mali. I am nine years old and I live in a village in northern Thailand with my grandparents, mom, dad, brothers and sisters. The monsoon rains bring lots of water from June until October. We need the water to grow our rice and vegetables. But it means we have to build our houses on poles to stay dry.

We live by a river where I fish with my grandfather, and near a forest where I pick fresh mangoes and watch for shy leaf monkeys in the trees. I like to write stories and make shadow puppets to put on shows for my family and friends. Most of all, I love elephants and helping to keep them safe.

Mali is making a *wai*

Welcome — Yindi Tonrap!
(Yin-ti-tawn-rap)

Yindi Tonrap means "Welcome" in Thai.

Tawan

My name is Tawan. My mom gave me the nickname *Ling Noi* (little monkey) because I used to climb on everything. She still calls me that even though I'm 11 years old now. It makes sense that monkeys are my favorite animals.

My favorite sport is *sepak takro*, which is like volleyball except that you can only use your feet. I also like making kites and I'm learning to play the *pi*, a traditional Thai instrument that is like an oboe.

I live with my parents and little brother Phoom (he's seven) in Bangkok. This is the capital of Thailand, with over 8.5 million people. My mom owns a business selling Thai crafts. My dad is a science teacher. Our school has kids from all over the world.

Bangkok has lots of traffic, but we use the subway, Skytrain, and boats to get around.

The most fun way (and noisiest!) is by *tuk tuk*, a three-wheeled motorcycle car. The name comes from the sputtering noises their engines make.

Mali

Thailand is in Southeast Asia. We say it is shaped like the head of an elephant—with a very long, skinny trunk! You might have to turn the book sideways to see it.

Thailand has really warm weather all year. But the northern mountains get a little colder during the winter. The three seasons are:

Cool or dry season: November to February

Hot season: March to May

Monsoon rainy season: June to October

Chiang Mai—capital of Northern Thailand and the former Kingdom of Lanna

Northern Thailand

The Thai Elephant Conservation Camp—near Lampang (where my uncle works)

Doi Intanon National Park—with beautiful waterfalls, the highest mountain in Thailand (8,415 feet or 2, 565 meters), and 362 kinds of birds

Central Thailand

Damnoen Saduak Floating Market (near Bangkok) where farmers sell their fruits and vegetables from boats

Monkey Training College near Surat Thani

Phuket—an island with beautiful beaches and lots of tourists

Southern Thailand

8

On The Map

Sukhothai—capital of an ancient Thai Kingdom with many interesting archeological sites

Isan

Lopburi—one of the oldest cities in Thailand and home to the monkey festival in November

Surin—home of the Elephant Roundup each November

Ayutthaya—capital of the Kingdom of Ayutthaya with famous temples and the face of Buddha encased by tree roots

Bangkok—the capital of Thailand (Tawan lives here!)

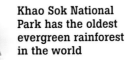

The Mekong River—the 12th longest river in the world (2,703 miles or 4,350 kilometers). It runs through six countries from China to Vietnam.

Khao Sok National Park has the oldest evergreen rainforest in the world

Northern Thailand (where Mali lives) is the elephant's ear. Hundreds of years ago, people migrated here from China. They called it the Kingdom of Lanna (1292-1775), which means "a thousand rice fields." And we still grow lots of rice here! There are huge mountains and forests surrounding beautiful valleys. Many groups of people, like the Karen, Hmong, Mien, Lahu, Akha, and Lisu, live in those mountains and have their own customs and languages. I have Hmong and Lisu friends at my school.

Isan, or northeastern Thailand, is the elephant's neck. This area was once part of neighboring Lao kingdoms. Many people in Isan speak Lao and eat Laotian food.

Central Thailand is the elephant's head. This is where the early Thai kingdoms of Sukhothai (1200-1350) and Ayutthaya (1350–1767) were located. Once called Siam, Thailand was created by uniting all the different kingdoms in 1767. The capital was moved from Ayutthaya to Thonburi on the Chao Phraya River. In 1782, the capital was moved across the river to Bangkok, which is the biggest and most important city in Thailand today.

Southern Thailand, the elephant's trunk, is a long isthmus. Part of the southern lands once belonged to kingdoms in Malaysia, but became part of Thailand in 1909. This area has forest and parks with interesting birds. It also has beautiful, warm beaches and many fishermen as well.

Great Places to Visit!

There are so many great places to go in Thailand, and lots to do!

Hill Tribe Villages near Chiang Mai and Chiang Rai

Many different peoples live in Northern Thailand, and all of them are interesting! Come and visit the hill tribe villages of the Karen, Hmong, Mien, Lahu, Htin, Akha, or Lisu. It's fun to learn about their customs, languages, music, dances and crafts. You can see the women weaving beautiful cloth on big looms. Or watch the men making jewelry, decorations, and tools.

A girl of the Karen tribe is weaving the cloth for which the tribe is famous. It is also famous for the long (and heavy!) brass coils that the women wear around their necks from the time they are five or six years old. They also wear brass rings on their forearms and shins.

Ban Bo Luang (Nan Province)

Ban Bo Luang means "salt-well village," and is in the mountains near Chiang Rai. This is a Htin hill tribe village that is known for—you guessed it—making salt! While most salt comes from the ocean, the salt in Ban Bo Luang is taken from wells in the village. Villagers collect brine (very salty water) from wells then boil it until salt crystals are formed. They dry the salt crystals in bamboo basketsand it is very pure and good to eat!

Baskets of salt suspended over a hot pan.

Kamphaeng Phet (Near Sukhothai)

Kamphaeng Phet is an ancient royal city that was part of the Sukhothai Kingdom over seven hundred years ago. The name means Diamond Wall, because long ago there was a very strong wall built around the city—as strong as diamonds! The United Nations named the city a World Heritage Site, because it is very important to the history of Thailand.

Temples in Chiang Mai often have a three-tiered roof like this one. Carvings of nagas or dragons stand guard over the temple. A naga is a god who takes the form of a cobra.

Chiang Mai (Northern Thailand)

Chiang Mai is the second largest city in the country and was the center of the Lanna Kingdom long ago. The city is in a valley surrounded by rice fields and mountains. You can still see parts of the old wall and moat that encircled the old city a thousand years ago. There are hundreds of beautiful temples and traditional homes made of teak. And there's lots to do, like visiting the great zoo, the tiger park, an orchid and butterfly farm, and the night bazaar.

A fun way to see the ancient ruins is to rent a bike or take a tuk tuk to visit the temples, Buddha statutes, and other cool buildings from the earliest days of the city. Be sure to look for Wat Chang Rop, which means "elephant encircled chedi" because the elephants are carved into the wall all the way around the base of the temple.

Elephants carved into the base of Wat Chang Rop

Kaeng Krachan National Park

Kaeng Krachan National Park is the largest of the 127 national parks in Thailand. It is located in a rain forest in southern Thailand. Two major rivers originate in the mountains in the park, creating beautiful waterfalls. The park is home to over 420 species of birds and 300 types of butterflies. There are also reptiles, insects and 57 kinds of mammals, such as leopards, bears, macaques, crab-eating mongoose, elephants…well, you get the idea.

The Long-tailed Broadbill is one of many fantastic birds you can see in Kaeng Krachan National Park.

Some of my favorites animals in the park are the green crested lizard, the spotted owl, and the great hornbill birds. The park has giant caves where horseshoe bats live, but all the bat guano in the caves can be pretty smelly! Look out for the many types of snakes that live in the park, like the Siamese cat snake and three kinds of python!

Stalagmites and stalactites in the limestone caves are not found only in Khrabi, but also along other parts of the southern coast, and on the island of Phuket as well.

Khrabi Boat Rides to Limestone Caves

Khrabi is a town on southern Thailand across the Gulf of Thailand from the beach resort island of Phukhet. Kids love to take boat tours—longtail boats, speed boats or kayaks—to explore the amazing network of limestone caves along the coast. Some of the caves contain really cool stalagmites and stalactites.

According to local folklore, many people believe certain caves are home to spirits and they leave items of worship as well as Buddha images. A number of the caves have prehistoric paintings, stone tools and pottery shards from the earliest people in the region. Plus you'll see all kinds of wildlife from monkeys to brightly colored crabs, fish, and birds.

Bangkok Children's Discovery Museum

At the Bangkok Children's Discovery Museum you can learn about the history and culture of Thailand, and also about dinosaurs, the human body and make bubbles from the inside out. In the Culture and Society Gallery, you can try on traditional Thai clothes, play Thai musical instruments and see exhibits on folk dancing and languages around the country. Outside, there's a fantastic playground with a fountain and water jets.

Ko Kret Island (Outside Bangkok)

Just a ferry ride from Bangkok, Ko Kret is a tiny island that became isolated after a canal was dug to make a shortcut in the Chao Phraya River. You could walk all the way around the island in about two hours—that's how small Ko Kret is! There aren't any roads or bridges, just paths leading to temples, villages and riverside houses built on wooden stilts. The only way to get to some parts of the island is by boat.

The leaning stupa of Wat Poramaiyikawat is a beautiful Buddhist temple on Koh Kret Island near Bangkok.

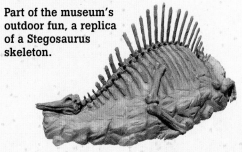

Part of the museum's outdoor fun, a replica of a Stegosaurus skeleton.

Ko Kret was settled by the Mon people two hundred years ago, a tribe that now mainly live in Burma. They are famous for terracotta pottery with intricate etchings and carvings, used for cooking a meal at the table. It's fun to watch the pots being made.
　　The weekend market here is always super busy. The stalls sell delicious Mon snacks, like boat noodles, fish cakes and sweets!

11

Let's Have Some Monkey Fun
(Ling Sanuk)

Monkeys like to have fun! You can see them all over Thailand. Some live to be 30 years old! They even get a starring role in folktales (like the Ramakien on page 44).

Tawan

It's a Party

I went to Lopburi last year for the biggest monkey party ever. Crab-eating macaques roam the streets, swing from roofs, and hop onto cars all year long, but they go wild in November. The town provides giant platters of fruit, peanuts, cucumbers, and raw crabs at the ancient Pra Prang Sam Yot temple. The monkeys go into an eating frenzy!

Monkey Business

On our summer vacation, we visited the Monkey Training College in Surat Thani. Pigtailed macaques learn how to climb coconut trees and knock down the ripest coconuts. After graduation, they work on plantations. Some can pick 1,000 coconuts a day. Now that's worth a banana or two! Most of their diet is made up of fruit, nuts and seeds, but they also eat small animals.

Thailand has 14 kinds of monkeys and apes (apes, such as gibbons, are larger than monkeys and don't have tails). Who can resist a Dusky Leaf Monkey (Spectacled Languar)?

Look, No Hands!
Sepak Takro—Thailand's Favorite Sport

To play, one team member throws the ball to the server who kicks it over the net. A team scores when the other team drops the ball, knocks it out of the court, or touches it with their hands. A set is 15 or 21 points, and a team must win two sets. Players make spectacular jumps to hit the ball. It's pretty exciting to watch—and even more exciting to play!

Some people think the game started in Malaysia while others say Indonesia. But Thailand adopted rules for sepak takro in 1829 and it's been a favorite sport ever since. Kids also play soccer with takro balls and hoop takro, where you have to kick the ball into a basketball hoop. Now that's tough!

*Rattan is thin strips from a palm tree.

Other Sports Kids Like

Soccer: Lots of kids play soccer in Thailand, only we call it football.

Muai Thai Kickboxing: This is a martial art that combines boxing and kicking. It helps kids learn self-defense and discipline. Kickboxing has been around a long time in Southeast Asia. You can watch professional kickboxing matches. There is even a special dance performed by kickboxers to show off their skills!

The *ram muay* dance

Special Thai Crafts
Silk Weaving, Lacquer Ware, Jewelry and...Umbrellas?

Thailand produces beautiful handmade crafts that are sold around the world (this is what Tawan's mother does). Many crafts are made in small villages like mine. Artists learn to make them at home from their family or neighbors.

Silk Cloth

I love to watch my grandmother weave silk cloth on her big wooden loom. Her beautiful fabric is sold in stores in Chiang Mai and Bangkok. Grandmother made me a silk outfit that I wear for Songkran (see page 28) and other special celebrations. Grandmother is teaching me to weave, but it's hard. I hope someday I can be as good as she is!

Step 1:
I help Grandmother raise thousands of little, squiggly silkworms that eat mulberry leaves and berries. After three to four weeks the worms spin their thick cocoons. It takes about 1,000 cocoons to make one silk shirt. That's a lot of worms!

Step 2:
We boil the cocoons (the poor worms are no more) to separate the fibers.

Step 3:
Grandmother unwinds tiny strands of silk from the cocoons and spins them into long threads. It takes 40 hours to make one small spindle of silk thread. Next, we soak the thread in cold water before dying the threads with bright colors made from plants growing near our village.

Lacquer Boxes and Figures

My grandfather is also an artist. He carves lovely boxes and figures, such as elephants and monkeys, from mango wood or teak wood. Then he paints them with many layers of lacquer, made from the sap of a mango tree. He etches patterns in the lacquer and fills the patterns with black or dark blue paint. Grandfather made me a beautiful elephant figure, since he knows I love elephants!

Gold and Silver Jewelry

In the mountains of northern Thailand peoples like the Hmong and Karen are known for their handmade gold and silver jewelry. They make necklaces, bracelets, earrings, and beads with special traditional designs. They sell their jewelry in the night markets in Chiang Mai and Bangkok. My friend Moua, who is Hmong, gave me a silver bracelet her father made with (can you guess?) an elephant!

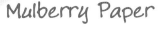

Mulberry Paper

Mulberry trees are useful for more than just feeding silkworms. My aunt collects the tree bark and soaks it in water. Then she beats it into a paste that she makes into paper. You can find picture frames, books, and other things made from Mulberry paper in stores in Thailand.

Painted Umbrellas

Thailand is hot most of the year. Everywhere you go you'll see people walking with umbrellas to stay out of the hot sun. Near Chiang Mai, villagers made hand-painted paper umbrellas in beautiful colors, painted with flowers, birds and other pictures.

Speak Thai with Me!
Learning a Few Words of Thai is Easy!

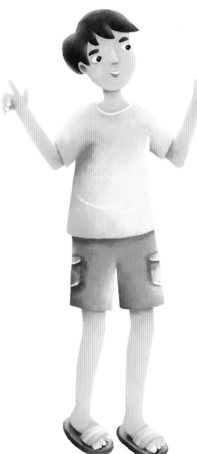

Our language is called Thai. It can be written in script (it might look like scribbles and curlicues if you're not used to it) or with the same letters used in English. Thai is spoken using five tones of the voice—high, medium, low, rising or falling. So you can say the same word using different tones and it has five different meanings! It can get confusing when you first start but once you get the hang of it, it's like music.

Try speaking some Thai words (you can hear these words spoken and find a pronunciation guide on this book's page at www.tuttlepublishing.com)

English	Thai Script	Thai in Latin-Based Spelling
Mother	แม่	**mae**[F]
Father	พ่อ	**pho**[F]
Sister	พี่สาว	**phi**[F] **sao**[R]
Brother	พี่ชาย	**phi**[F] **chai**[M]
House	บ้าน	**ban**[F]
Dog	สุนัข	**su**[L]**-nak**[H]
Cat	แมว	**maeo**[M]
School	โรงเรียน	**rong**[M] **rian**[M]
Song	เพลง	**phleng**[M]
Game	เกม	**kem**[M]
Flower	ดอกไม้	**dok**[L] **mai**[H]
Food	อาหาร	**aa**[M]**-han**[R]
One	หนึ่ง	**neung**[L]
Two	สอง	**song**[R]
Three	สาม	**sam**[R]
Four	สี่	**si**[L]
Five	ห้า	**ha**[F]

L=low tone, M=mid tone, H=high tone, F=falling tone, R=rising tone

Little Mali Has a Cat

Nu Mali Mi Luk Maeo Miao

Arranged by Elaine Russell

Nu   Mali   mi   luk   maeo   miao
Little   Mali   has   a   little   cat

Luk   maeo   miao   luk   maeo   miao
little   cat   little   cat

Nu   Mali   mi   luk   maeo   miao
Little   Mali   has   a   little   cat

luk   maeo   miao   tu   yai
Little   cat   is   big

This song shows how many Thai words sound similar. *Nu Mali Mi Luk Maeo Miao* mean "Little Mali has a little cat." The word for cat is based on the "meow" sound the cat makes.

17

Thai Elephants (Chang)
Gentle Giants

These animals are loyal, brave, really smart, and HUGE.

Mali

My uncle is an elephant trainer at the Thai Elephant Conservation Center near our village. The center is sponsored by the King and Queen of Thailand. The King's white elephants live here in the Royal Stable. I love to pet the baby elephants and give them sticks of sugar cane.

Rocking in the Band: The Thai Elephant Orchestra plays drums, gongs, pipes, and horns. (You can buy a CD or MP3 of their hit songs www.mulatta.org/thaieleorch.html or on the Thai Elephant Conservation Center site above)

The Next Picasso: Elephants can paint pictures, holding the brush in their trunks. Their trainers dip the brushes in the paint.

Score that Goal: Elephants love playing soccer, kicking the ball, and scoring a goal.

Long ago in Thailand, elephants carried warriors into battle, hauled logs from the forests, and plowed rice fields. Today machines do this work, but elephants will always be important. These big guys still have a few tricks up their trunks!

The Surin Elephant Roundup

Where do 200 elephants go to show off? Last November I went with my uncle's family to the Surin Elephant Roundup in the Isan region. Elephants and their mahouts come from all parts of Thailand to demonstrate their skills at playing soccer and lifting logs. The big finish is an exciting reenactment of a battle that took place in the Burmese Siamese War hundreds of years ago.

Lights, Camera, Action: Elephants get important roles in Thai movies and live performances.

Did You Know?

- Asian elephants have smaller ears and are three feet shorter than African elephants.
- Asian elephants can live for 70 to 80 years.
- The skin of an Asian elephant is an inch thick.
- The elephants only eat plants and love mangoes.
- White, or albino, elephants are rare and thought to bring good luck, but only the king can own them.

Delicious Thai Foods
Streetside Food Carts are Common in Thailand

My mom gives Phoom and me some *baht* (Thai money) so we can get a snack after school at one of the food carts lining the streets of Bangkok. You can get everything here!

Meals on a bamboo stick: tropical fruits, grilled meats and sausage, fish balls, grilled shrimp, sliced hard-boiled eggs—even ice cream

Most kids have tried fruits like papaya, pineapple and coconut, but have you heard of these? They are sweet and yummy!

Rambutans

Custard Apples

Longan

Rose Apples

Dragonfruit

Durian—Watch out, this is really strong. Some people say it smells like a sewer!! It tastes really good though—really! You just have to get over the smell.

Thai cooking uses hot chilies (the hotter the better for me!), lemon grass, fish sauce, spicy vinegar, lime juice, curry paste, and cilantro (also called coriander leaves). Try making the recipes on the next page. I bet you'll like them!

20

Steaming bowls of soup or freshly cooked meat and vegetables on rice

Whipped fruit drinks or tea with sweet milk, served in a plastic bag with a straw

Do you like insects? How about these snacks—fried grasshoppers with soy sauce, bee larvae, or crushed beetle paste?

Chicken Satay

Combine all the following ingredients in a large bowl:

REMEMBER!
Always get your parents' permission and supervision when cooking and using sharp utensils.

½ cup coconut milk
1 Tbsp. lime juice
1 tsp. curry powder
1 tsp. ground ginger
  (or 1 Tbsp. fresh grated ginger)
1 clove garlic crushed
Dash of salt and pepper

Prepare the chicken strips below and add the spices to a bowl to marinate for two hours:

• 1 large boneless, skinless chicken breast (two halves) sliced into strips about 1-inch (2 cm) wide by 4 or 5 inches (10 cm) long and ½ inch (1 cm) thick
• Soak wooden skewers in water for 20 minutes before putting the chicken strips on them.
• Barbeque the chicken on a hot grill or grill pan for 5 to 7 minutes, turning once to cook both sides

Thai Peanut Sauce

For dipping grilled chicken or shrimp skewers or fresh vegetables

Makes 1 ⅓ cups of peanut sauce.

1 cup creamy peanut butter
⅓ cup coconut milk
2 Tbsp water
2 Tbsp lime
2 Tbsp soy sauce
¾ tsp fish sauce
1 tsp hot sauce
1 garlic, minced
2 Tbsp cilantro chopped

Stir all the ingredients together thoroughly and put in serving bowl. Just add some grilled chicken or shrimp skewers and cut up vegetables, such as carrots, peppers, celery, snow peas, and jicama. It's a great peanut taste!

The Girl Who Spoke in Flowers
A Traditional Thai Folktale

Once there was a beautiful girl called Phikul, named after the gold-colored flowers of the bulletwood tree. After her father died, she lived with her step-mother and step-sister, Fah. Phikul was sweet and kind, but her step-mother and Fah were jealous and mean. They forced Phikul to do all the hard work. She had to feed the chickens and pigs, work in the fields, pound the rice, wash the clothes, and cook the meals. One day Phikul went to fetch water from the nearby stream. As she carried her buckets home, an old, bent-over woman wearing torn clothes, appeared. She asked for some water. Phikul gave her cupful after cupful.

The old woman said, "You are gentle and kind. Even though I am poor and shabby, you treat me nicely. I will give you a gift. Whenever you feel sympathy for someone, phikul flowers will flow from your mouth." Then the old woman disappeared. Phikul knew she must be a kind forest spirit who had come to help her.

> I love the Thai story called *Phikul Thong*. It's about a girl and her evil step-mother and step-sister. Maybe it will remind you of a story you know.

Mali

22

When Phikul got home her step-mother scolded her for being late. Phikul told her about the old woman. As she spoke, flowers poured from her mouth. The greedy step-mother quickly changed her mood and encouraged Phikul to speak more.

The step-mother collected as many of the gold-colored flowers as she could and sold them in the market. Phikul was forced to speak all day so more flowers would come from her mouth.

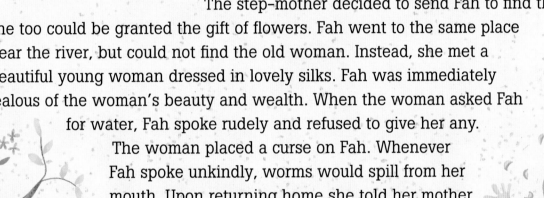

After a week Phikul's throat was so sore that she couldn't speak. Her step-mother hit her, but Phikul could not utter a word.

The step-mother decided to send Fah to find the old woman so she too could be granted the gift of flowers. Fah went to the same place near the river, but could not find the old woman. Instead, she met a beautiful young woman dressed in lovely silks. Fah was immediately jealous of the woman's beauty and wealth. When the woman asked Fah for water, Fah spoke rudely and refused to give her any.

The woman placed a curse on Fah. Whenever Fah spoke unkindly, worms would spill from her mouth. Upon returning home she told her mother what had happened. Her angry words filled the house with worms.

The step-mother thought Phikul had lied about the old woman so that Fah would be cursed. She beat Phikul and drove her away from the house.

Phikul's heart ached. She missed her father and the happy life she had known before he died. She ran into the forest and found shelter under a tree, where she cried and cried. A short time later, a young prince rode into the forest. He saw Phikul crying and asked what had happened. By the time she finished her tale, the forest was full of gold-colored flowers. The prince fell in love with her at once. The couple married and ruled the kingdom. They lived a long and happy life.

Let's Play a Game
Here Are Some Fun Games Us Kids Like to Play in Thailand

Mali

Here are some fun Thai games I play with my sisters, brothers, and friends. Maybe you play some games like these.

Duck and Goose (Mon Son Pha)

This game starts with a group of kids sitting in a circle. One person is picked to be Mon. Mon walks slowly around the circle with a cloth, and drops it behind another player. The chosen player picks up the cloth and chases Mon around the circle. Mon tries to get to the empty spot and sit down before the player can tag them. If they make it, the player with the cloth becomes the new Mon.

Crow Hatches Eggs (I Ka Fak Khai)

Start by drawing a big circle on the ground large enough to fit all the players. Inside that, draw a smaller circle for only one person. Each player puts a marble, a piece of paper marked with their name, or a small stone inside the inner circle. These are the eggs. One person is the crow and stands in the small circle. The crow uses their arms and legs to try to block other players from stealing the eggs.

The other players try to grab the eggs without touching the crow or stepping in the small circle. And they must stay inside the larger circle. When all the eggs are stolen, the crow covers their eyes and counts to 20. The other players hide their eggs nearby—maybe behind a tree or wall. The crow must hunt for the eggs. The owner of the first egg the crow finds becomes the next crow. Everyone collects the eggs, and a new game starts.

Snake Eats Tail (Ngu Kin Hang)

Pick one father snake and one mother snake. Everyone else lines up behind the mother snake and holds the waist of the person in front of them. As the mother and babies sway side to side, Father snake calls out, "Which well do you drink from?" Mother snake answers, "I drink from a well in the stone." The mother and babies call out together, "We do too." The father says what part of the mother snake he will bite (the end or middle) and begins to chase after the babies. The mother puts her arms out to block the father as the line of babies runs to keep out of the father's reach. When the father tags one of the babies, they are out. The game is over after the father tags all the babies.

One-Legged Rabbit (Kratai Kha Diao)

Form two teams of equal size: one team of rabbits and a second team of players. Then mark off a square large enough for the second team to stand inside and move around. The rabbits stand outside the square. One rabbit at a time hops on one leg into the square and tries to tag as many of the second team as they can. Players inside the square are out if they are tagged or if they cross the boundary by mistake.

A rabbit is out if they put their other foot down or change legs. If a rabbit gets tired, they can hop back out and ask another rabbit to take their place. The game is over when all the players in the square are tagged out, or if all the rabbits are out first.

The Story of Ta-in and Ta-na
A Fishy Tale of Two Friends

Two best friends named Ta-in and Ta-na live in a Thai fishing village. They built a small boat and fish together in the sea. Each day they cast their nets into the water and catch plenty of fish. But over time the fish begin to disappear.

One day Ta-in and Ta-na try every fishing spot they know but without success. Ta-in finally snags one fish. When they get home, Ta-in says, "I caught this fish so I will take the head and middle. You can have the tail."

Ta-na frowned. "But I want the head and middle too."

A terrible argument erupts. The friends grow angrier and angrier until, finally, they shout and push each other. Villagers come running to see what is wrong.

Ta-yoo, the village elder, pulls them apart. "Stop this fighting! Tell me the problem, and I will solve it." Ta-in and Ta-na explain about the fish. Ta-yoo thinks a long time as the villagers wait to hear his solution.

I share a bedroom with my brother Phoom. He's messy and always asks to use my things. My mom says sharing is important and reminds me about the story of Ta-in and Ta-na.

Tawan

"Ta-in, you caught the fish so you take the head," Ta-yoo says at last. "Ta-na, you get the tail. Because I solved the problem, I'll take the middle of the fish."

The friends were speechless, but nodded in agreement. Ta-yoo hands them the head and tail then takes the biggest and best part of the fish for himself. Ta-in and Ta-na stare unhappily at their pieces of fish.

"I should not have been so selfish," Ta-in says.

"No, I was the selfish one," says Ta-na.

"We were both greedy," Ta-in said, shaking his head. "We both lost today."

From then on the friends work together and share everything. When lots of fish return to the sea near their village, Ta-in and Ta-na have plenty to eat and make lots of money. They had learned a valuable lesson: it's always best to share, in good times and bad.

27

Songkran Water Days
The Thai New Year's Celebration

S uk san wan Songkran!—this is how kids say "Happy Songkran Day" on the Thai New Year. This is the biggest holiday in Thailand, lasting for three days (April 13-15) – and in some places even longer!

Songkran is referred to as the "Water Days" because this when we pour water on everything. The water washes away all our troubles from the past year so we can start the New Year afresh. My family begins by cleaning our apartment from top to bottom.

The first day of Songkran is National Elderly Day and the second day is National Family Day. Many people who live in the city go to visit their family in the village. We spend time with my grandparents in Bangkok. My brother and I sprinkle rose-scented water on their hands to show our respect, and they wish us good luck in the New Year.

My brother and I like to bring sand to make a stupa, a type of temple. The sand is meant to return to the temple the dirt we carried out on our shoes during the past year. We decorate the stupa with prayer flags, flowers, and leaves. They sell Sonkran flags at stores, but we like to make our own (see how on page 31)

We also celebrate Songkran at our Buddhist temple. My family brings food and other offerings for Buddha and the monks (learn about Buddhism on page 38). The monks wash the temple Buddhas and give blessings. Then we pour water on the Buddhas and sprinkle the monks with rose-scented water to honor them.

Water, Water Everywhere!

Besides the ceremonies and family time, what kids love best about Songkran is the ultimate water fight! We get to dump buckets of water, blast our super soakers and throw colored chalk powder on our friends. Pretty soon everyone is covered in powder and dripping wet, but it feels good since April is the hottest month of the year. There is no way to stay dry if you go outside on Songkran!

I also like the big parades during the daytime and huge fireworks at night. It's all great fun!

Other New Year's Celebrations

People from many different countries and backgrounds live in Thailand and celebrate other New Year as well. Here are just a few:

Western New Year on December 31st: There are fireworks and parties, as we say *sawat di pi mai* (Happy New Year).

Hmong New Year in late November: A celebration of the rice harvest with three days of festivities, including dancing, games, and bull races.

Chinese New Year in January or February: This includes the big paper lion parade along with lots of music and fireworks.

Awal Muharram, Islamic New Year in Southern Thailand: The date changes according to the Islamic calendar. This is mostly a religious day spent praying at the mosques.

29

Make a Wish for the Thai New Year
Songkran Is Not Just for Water Fights—We Make Stupas and Flags Too!

The stupas we make are modeled on monuments like this one in Wat Puag Hong, Chiang Mai. These originated as places of burial. With the spread of Buddhism they became houses for relics and texts that symbolized the Buddha's enlightenment. There are Buddhism's earliest religious monument.

Make a Sand Stupa and Prayer Flags

Here's how you can make a sand stupa and prayer flags to celebrate Songkran. (You might want to do this project outside.) You can make either a triangle-shaped flag or a longer banner flag. Or both!

Supplies

A square piece of cardboard about 2 feet (60 cm) wide
Plastic wrap
Construction paper in different colors
Scissors
Crayons, colored markers or ink stamps
Glue or clear tape
Bamboo skewers or wooden chopsticks
Small flowers and leaves for decoration
6 to 8 cups of sand (or more if you want)
Water to moisten sand (about 1½ cups)

To Make the Prayer Banners

1. Cut out triangle-shaped flags (like a baseball pennant) about 4" (10 cm) wide and 7" (18 cm) long. For a banner flag, cut out a strip of paper about 4" (10 cm) wide and 12" (30.5 cm) long.

2. Decorate the flags with patterns or drawings, using markers, crayons and stamps.

3. Fold one end of the banner around a bamboo skewer and glue or tape it in place.

To Make the Sand Stupas

1. Cover the cardboard with plastic wrap and tape it in place. Place the sand in a plastic bowl and mix with water until it can hold a shape. Press it down to make the mixture compact. Put the cardboard on top of bowl and turn it over then remove the bowl so you get a mound of sand on the base.

2. Shape the sand into a stupa with multiple tiers—each one smaller as you work your way to the top.

3. Decorate the mound of sand with your banners, fresh flowers and leaves.

Eating Rice with Every Meal
Do You Like Rice? Every Thai Person Loves Rice!

Mali

I eat rice (*khao*) at every meal—either rice noodles or cooked rice. So does everyone I know! It's not surprising that rice is the biggest crop grown in Thailand. When Mom calls out, "Kin khao!" it's the same as saying "Come to dinner!" But this actually means, "Eat rice!" That's how important rice is to us.

My family works hard during the rice growing season. I help after school and on days off. In late May, my father and brother Saifa dig up the ground with a plow pulled by our water buffalo. Then everyone helps scatter rice seeds on part of the plowed land. The monsoon rains soon flood the land, or rice paddies.*

My friends and I love to play and swim in the water around the paddies. Walking in the thick mud makes wonderful sloshy noises!

Six to eight weeks after planting, we pull up the young sprouts and replant them in the rest of our paddies so they have more room to grow. In October, when the plants are fully grown, the whole family helps to cut and gather the stalks. Sometimes we get a week off from school to help with the harvest. Dad, Mom and Saifa use a tool called a *khiao*, a type of sickle, or curved knife. Dad says next year we'll buy a combine machine. It's a type of tractor with blades in the front that turn and cut down the rice stalks.

The rice grains are threshed, or beaten, off the stalks, and spread out to dry in the sun for a few days. Then it's off to the mill to have the brown covers, or hulls, removed from the rice grains. The hulled white rice is stored in 100 pound (45.5 kilogram) sacks. There will be plenty for our family to eat and sell at the market! It's not all work, though. We have fun during the rice season too!

*Paddy is a Malaysian word for flooded land

The Royal Plowing Ceremony

My family went to Bangkok last May to watch the 700-year-old Royal Plowing Ceremony, a national holiday. The king gave a blessing to ensure a good rice crop. Two royal oxen plowed a dirt field in front of the Royal Palace. Then the Minister of Agriculture spread rice seeds in the field.

After the ceremony, the other kids and I sifted through the dirt to collect royal seeds. I found 22 seeds! I got to plant my own rice paddy. It was small but very special. And the rice I produced was the best ever!

Rocket Festival (Bun Bang Fai)

This festival also takes place in May. Everyone dresses in their best clothes and parades through our village with decorated platforms that carry rockets (big fireworks). The Buddhist monks say a blessing for a good rice crop. My friends and I love to dance to the music and eat all the good food our moms cook.

Later in the day, villagers fire rockets into the sky. According to an ancient tale, the rockets, or *bang fai*, are sent to ask the rain god for plenty of rain to grow our rice. Cover your ears— the rockets are really loud!

Honoring the Rice Goddess
Delicious Thai Recipes You Can Make at Home With Your Parents

At different times in the rice growing season, we give thanks to the rice goddess, Mae Pra Posop, so she will give the paddies a big harvest. We build small platforms by the rice fields and leave her offerings of banana, limes, and sugar cane.

Sticky Rice with Mangos

My favorite dessert! Sticky rice is just what it sounds like—rice that sticks together. (Note: sticky rice is also called sweet rice or glutinous rice, and can be found in many grocery stores and Asian markets.)

Serves 8-10 people

1½ cups uncooked sticky rice
2 cups water
¼ teaspoon salt
2 teaspoons tapioca or corn starch
2 cans coconut milk
1 cup + 1 tablespoon sugar
2-3 fresh ripe mangos, peeled, pitted and sliced

REMEMBER! Always get your parents' permission and supervision when cooking and using sharp utensils.

You might like to try some of my favorite foods. My mother taught me how to cook these recipes.

1. Bring the rice and water to a boil in a large saucepan then turn the heat down. Cover and simmer on very low heat about 15-20 minutes until the water is all absorbed.

2. While the rice is cooking, place 1½ cups coconut milk, 1 cup sugar, and ½ teaspoon salt in a saucepan and cook over medium heat; bring to a boil for a minute and stir to melt the sugar, then remove from heat.

3. Stir the cooked rice into coconut milk mixture and place in a glass dish about 7 x 11 inches (18 x 28 centimeters). Cover and let cool 1 hour to absorb all the coconut milk.

fresh ripe mangos

sticky rice

4. Make the sauce by mixing together ¾ cup coconut milk, 1-2 tablespoons sugar, ¼ teaspoon salt, and 2 teaspoons tapioca or corn starch in a saucepan; stir constantly until it reaches a boil and thickens. Remove from heat and let cool.

5. Serve squares of the rice with mango slices and sauce over the top. Yum yum!

Mali

Thai Chicken Noodle Soup

This is a tasty dish made from rice noodles. You can eat it at any time of day, but I like it best for breakfast.

Serves 6

6 cups chicken broth

1 large carrot sliced
2 half chicken breasts, chopped into small pieces
2 bunches bok choy chopped
1 stalk lemongrass, minced
1 tomato, chopped
1 bay leaf
½ cup cilantro, chopped
Small piece of fresh ginger, grated
2 cloves garlic, diced
2 tablespoons each of fish sauce, Thai chili sauce,
  and lime juice
8-10 ounces flat rice noodles
Salt

1. In a large soup pot, bring chicken and stock to a boil over high heat. Add all the vegetables except bok choy. Cover and simmer for 15 minutes then add bok choy, fish sauce, chili sauce, and lime juice. Stir well and simmer covered for 5 minutes more.

2. While soup cooks, bring a large pot of salted water almost to a boil. Add the noodles. Remove from heat and let soak 5-8 minutes, or until soft but still chewy. Drain and rinse briefly with cold water to keep from sticking.

3. To serve, place a big mound of noodles in each bowl and top with the hot soup.

Besides rice, these recipes include some interesting foods you'll find in lots of Thai meals.

Lemon grass

This is a stalk that has a lemony smell and taste. It adds a special flavor to soups, meats and fish. The taste is hard to miss! Lemon grass is also used in teas to treat different kinds of ailments. Lemon grass grows in many parts of Asia and is used in more and more dishes worldwide, so it's not too hard to find in stores.

Fresh Ginger root

This looks very different from the pickled ginger you see in jars. Fresh ginger root is a golden yellow color inside. Its flavor is tangy and just a little sharp. It's used in cooking, baking and teas everywhere in the world. It's even great in ice cream!

Bok Choy (or Pak Choy)

This leafy vegetable is great both cooked and in salads and it's good for you too! It comes in different varieties, from the slightly sweeter and more tender baby bok choy to other varieties that can be a little more bitter. It's most commonly eaten in China, but it's used in lots of Thai dishes as well.

Coconut milk

This staple in Thai kitchens is made by grinding the coconut meat with a little water and then squeezing it to make a thick cream. It's a long process, though, and you can buy it canned in stores. (It is different from coconut water, however, that is a drink from inside the coconut—also delicious!) Coconut milk is used in soups and curry dishes. And, of course, we love it in sweet dishes too!

When Kids Rule!
National Children's Day in Thailand

E very second Saturday in January is National Children's Day in Thailand. Kids all over the country get to visit fun places for free or half-price. Kids even ride the bus for free (and the Skytrain and subway in Bangkok)! There are so many great places to visit, including zoos, museums, crocodile farms, elephant camps and national parks. Cities and villages hold special events like dog shows and boat rides. Government buildings are open for guided tours.

A Thai Proverb
Children are the future of the nation;
if the children are intelligent, the country will be prosperous.

This year my parents took Phoom and me to a special show of the Royal Thai Air Force. I got to sit in the cockpits of a helicopter and a fighter jet. I'd like to be a pilot when I'm older. Phoom really liked the firemen who dressed him up in their gear and let him spray a fire hose. I wish every day could be Children's Day!

Many People—Many Beliefs
The Thai People are Mainly Buddhists, But Not All Are...

Tawan

My dad tells me that the people who came to live in Thailand hundreds of years ago brought their religions and beliefs with them. My family is Buddhist, but at school, I have friends who follow other religions. Dad says that we should all try to recognize the beliefs our religions have in common, and respect the differences.

Buddhism

Buddhism began about 2,500 years ago in India when the teachings of a man named Siddhārtha Gautama spread through Asia. Over time, people in different areas developed their own ways of practicing Buddhism. Most people in Thailand and Southeast Asia (including my family) are Theraveda Buddhists. We follow the Buddha's teachings and honor our Buddhist monks. Lots of Chinese-Thais who live here follow Mahayana Buddhism. They believe there were many Buddhas and follow other teachings, called sutras, as well.

My family goes to a Buddhist temple, or *wat*, where we pray and make offerings. We also try to live in a way that brings love and kindness into the world. We believe that when you die you are born again, and your new life depends on what you still need to learn to reach enlightenment, which is a perfect understanding of life. Our idea of heaven is a state of joy and freedom called nirvana. Once we reach nirvana, we no longer need to be reborn. Since I like monkeys so much, I wonder if I was ever a monkey in one of my previous lives?

Sometimes on Sundays, I go with my grandmother at six in the morning (even though it's hard to get up!) to bring food to the monks as they walk down the street in their orange robes carrying bowls. There are lots of ceremonies and fun holiday festivals at our temple during the year.

The most famous Buddhist temple In Thailand is the Wat Phra Kaew next to the Royal Palace in Bangkok. Jewels, gold and colorful tiles cover the outside of the temple and scary-looking demon statues stand guard. The temple holds the beautiful Emerald Buddha, which is carved from jade. The inside walls are painted with beautiful murals of scenes from the Ramakien. (page 44)

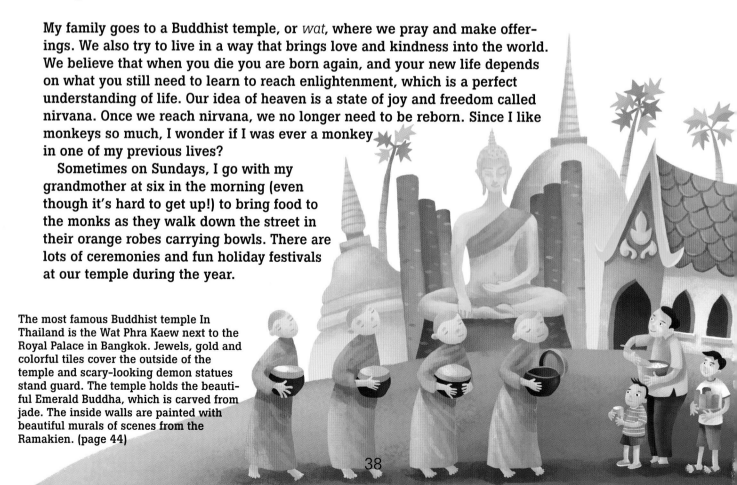

National Buddhist Holidays in Thailand

Makha Puja honors the day Buddha passed his wisdom to his followers before he died. (February)

Songkran is the Thai New Year, which is also a Buddhist celebration. (April)

Vesak celebrates the birth, enlightenment, and deathof Buddha. (May)

Asalha Puja honors the day of Buddha's first sermon. (July)

Vassa, also called the "Rains Retreat" because it takes place during the rainy season, is a period of study and meditation for monks. Laypeople often treat it like Lent in the Christian tradition and give up things like sweets and video games

Animism and Ancestor Worship

Many people in Thailand, including Buddhists and groups like the Hmong and Karen, worship the spirits of their ancestors and of the earth, such as the sky, water and trees. This is called animism. Like most people, my family has a spirit house, or *san phru pham*, outside our apartment building to give the spirits a home. We leave food and flowers and light incense and candles for the spirits, asking them to protect us. There are also spirit houses outside most businesses.

Spirit houses remind us to respect nature and our ancestors.

Hinduism

The Hindu religion began in India about 5,000 years ago and was practiced in Thailand before Buddhism became the main religion. Hindus believe in one God, Brahma, who also appears in the form of other gods and goddesses at different times, such as Vishnu, Shiva and Ganesha (the elephant god). Like Buddhists, Hindus believe that you are reborn after you die and must work to find the answer to life to end this cycle.

Ganesha is a very well-known god.

Islam

Islam began about 1,500 years ago in what is now Saudi Arabia. Muslims (people who practice Islam) pray to God, whom they call Allah, in mosques. They follow the teachings of the prophet Muhammad as written in their sacred book, the Quran. Islam was adopted as the main religion in many countries, including Indonesia and Malaysia. Most people who came from Malaysia to live in southern Thailand are Muslims.

Muslims stop and pray five times each day.

The Floating Lantern Festival
Loi Krathong

Kids love the beautiful *Loi Krathong*, or Floating Lantern Festival, that happens each November during the full moon. *Loi* means to float, and *Krathong* means little boat of banana leaves. We sail small boats with lighted candles down rivers and canals to honor Buddha and ask the Goddess of Water, Phra Mae Khongkha, to bring plenty of water for growing our rice the next year. The boats also carry away our bad luck from the past year.

The boats are decorated to look like a lotus blossom. At school we make boats in the traditional way with thick round slices of banana tree branches at the base. This is wrapped in banana leaves. We decorate it with more leaves and flowers, and add a candle, incense and a small coin in the middle of the flowers. Sometimes I add something personal. It is very exciting to put my boat in the water and watch it float away as I make my wishes to Buddha and the Goddess of Water.

As the bad luck of the past year floats away, we also let go of mistakes and start fresh. This lovely song speaks of the Buddhist concept of "making merit." Merit is made when we accumulate good thoughts and deeds, and treat each other with compassion.

40

The Floating Lantern Festival Song

Arrangement by Elaine Russell

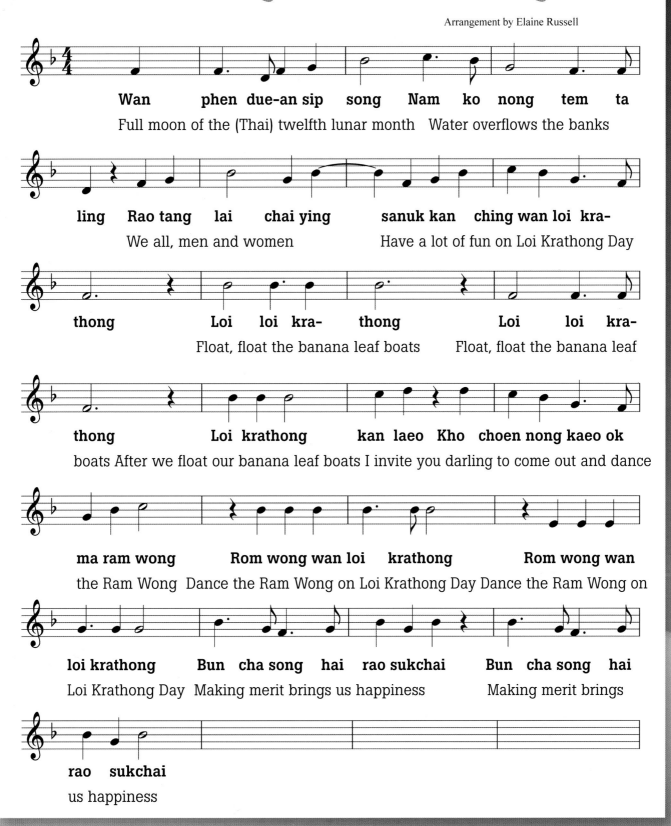

Wan phen due-an sip song Nam ko nong tem ta
Full moon of the (Thai) twelfth lunar month   Water overflows the banks

ling Rao tang lai chai ying sanuk kan ching wan loi kra-
We all, men and women   Have a lot of fun on Loi Krathong Day

thong Loi loi kra- thong Loi loi kra-
Float, float the banana leaf boats   Float, float the banana leaf

thong Loi krathong kan laeo Kho choen nong kaeo ok
boats After we float our banana leaf boats I invite you darling to come out and dance

ma ram wong Rom wong wan loi krathong Rom wong wan
the Ram Wong Dance the Ram Wong on Loi Krathong Day Dance the Ram Wong on

loi krathong Bun cha song hai rao sukchai Bun cha song hai
Loi Krathong Day Making merit brings us happiness   Making merit brings

rao sukchai
us happiness

Make Your Own Lantern Boat!

You can make your own Loi Krathong boat to celebrate the holiday just like we do in Thailand! You can go to a local river or pond, light your candle and incense, and set the boat adrift, Be sure to make some special wishes!

Supplies

1 round paper maché box (7½ inch across and 3 inches deep—or 19 by 8 cm—available at craft stores)
7½ inch round of corkboard
Green construction paper
Pink construction paper
Fresh flowers in season (optional)
Glue
Double-sided tape
Ruler and pencil
Scissors

1.

Glue corkboard to the bottom of the paper maché box.

2.

Cut out green construction paper to cover sides and top of box and glue on.

3.

Cut out paper petals and glue them to the side of box with the top 1/3 of the petals standing above the top of box.

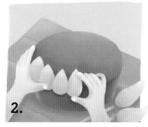

4.

Add fresh flowers or make a large lotus flower. (Cut out petals, bend at bottom, and glue to a small round base, alternating white and pink. Petals should stand up.)

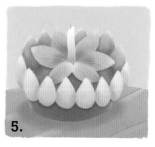

5.

Add a small candle in the middle, securing it with double-sided tape. If you like, use tape to add incense, a penny or nickel, and anything special you want to offer to the water goddess (like a special rock or shell).

The Flying Lanterns Festival (Yi-Peng)

Here in the north of Thailand, we celebrate the Lanna festival, Yi-Peng, at the same time as Loi Krathong. On this Buddhist holiday we send lanterns off into the sky to make merit and to carry our hopes and wishes to Buddha to be answered.

My dad and I make a *khom loi* (flying lantern) with a bamboo frame covered with rice paper. We light a big candle in the center and the heat lifts the lantern into the air. Magic fills the night as hundreds of tiny lights in the Loi Krathang boats twinkle across the water and the glowing Yi-Peng lanterns float up to join the stars!

Lanterns rise to the sky at Wiang Thakan at Thakan Village, Tumbol Barn Klang, San Patong District.

43

The Ramakien Story
Thailand's Most Famous Folk Story

The most famous folktale in all of Thailand, our national epic, is the Ramakien. This story is so amazing that kids never tire of it. It's all about the good guys versus the bad guys—gods and goddesses transformed into people and animals along with evil, scary demons, monsters and ogres. The tale is full of countless twists and magic to surprise you at every turn. Not to mention the awesome battles. Every time you think the good guys are safe, something else happens to put them in danger. Will they escape? Who will win in the end?

Tawan

The story is based on the Ramayana, a tale that came from India, but it was rewritten to become a Thai story. Most kids in Thailand know it as a marionette or shadow puppet play (more on page 52) or as a *khon* dance show (more on page 48). The incredible costumes and action make the Ramakien something you never forget. It takes a whole book to retell all of the Ramakien, so I'll explain about the four coolest characters and tell one small part of the story involving my absolute favorite, the monkey general, Hanuman.

Hanuman

This is the son of the God of Wind, who has eight arms and is often portrayed as having several heads. As a god, Hanuman can fly and exhale stars, suns and moons into the air. But on earth he is transforms into a small, white monkey, General of the Monkey Army. Hanuman joins Phra Ram to rescue Sida from Totsagan and defeat the demons of Longka. His small size fools his enemies into thinking he is harmless, but he surprises them with his immense powers.

Phra Ram

This was the god Phra Narai before being reborn as the human prince, Phra Ram, son of the King of Ayutthaya. The gods want him to get rid of Nontuk. Phra Ram visits Nontuk and transforms himself into a graceful dancer. Nontuk tries to imitate his dance moves but accidently points his deadly finger at himself, killing himself. The handsome, brave hero, Phra Ram, meets beautiful Princess Sida. They fall in love and marry. But there isn't any happily-ever-after yet!

Totsagan

This guy is king of the demon kingdom of Longka. On his head he carries nine more heads and 20 arms. In a prior life he was Nontuk, a trusted gatekeeper to the heavens. The gods gave him a magical power—a jeweled finger that could kill just by pointing at someone. But he betrays the gods by using the finger to kill gods and humans for his own gain, so the gods ask Phra Ram to stop him. When Phra Ram's efforts result in Nontuk's death, he is reborn as Totsagan, and he's out for revenge. This guy is really bad news!

Princess Sida

This beautiful princess doesn't know it, but she is actually the daughter of Totsagan. When she was born, Totsagan's brother said he had learned in a dream that Sida would bring about the end of Longka. So Totsagan sends the baby away. She is found and raised by the kind King Chanok until she marries Phra Ram. Later she is kidnapped by Totsagan. Phra Ram must rescue her with the help of the monkey general, Hanuman.

Here is one of my favorite episodes from the Ramakien. Hanuman and his men are going to Longka to tell the captured Princess Sida not to give up hope, she will be freed.

Tawan

General Hanuman—the Monkey King—and his men pushed their way through the deep forest for four long days before making the steep climb to the snowcapped peaks of the Hematiwan Mountains. They were tired and hungry, but their mission was too important for them to worry about these things. They must let Sida know they would soon be there to rescue her.

"We will sleep here tonight in the caves." Hanuman said to his men. "Tomorrow you can gather food and rest. I will fly over the ocean and discover how we can make our way to the island of Longka. We must find a way to build a bridge to the island so our armies can invade."

In the early morning light, Hanuman bid his men farewell. "I shall return within a day. Do not worry for my safety." He took on the form of a bird and soared into the sky in the direction of Longka.

The hideous she-demon, Pee Sua Samut, guardian of the island of Longka, lurked below the bubbling ocean waves. She scanned the sky for danger and saw Hanuman soaring above. Her angry eyes smoldered like hot coals, and she gnashed her great teeth. As Hanuman grew near, she sprang into the air, swinging a club and giving a fierce roar.

Hanuman darted to the side, barely escaping her club. Pee Sua Samut swung again, and again Hanuman managed to duck just in time. He quickly determined his sword was no match for this enormous monster. He had only one chance to defeat her. When the demon opened her great jaws once more and let loose another deafening roar, Hanuman flew directly into her mouth. He circled around her head like a bumblebee in a pot and slipped down into her stomach. Hanuman swung his sword in all directions, carving up the demon's insides, then tumbled back out of her mouth. The monster collapsed in the sea, lifeless, as the waters turned red. Pee Sua Samut would no longer be a problem!

Dancing Thai Style!
Learning Classical Dance Steps is Easy and Fun

Mali

When I grow up, I want to be a classical *lokorn nai* dancer. My mom took me to see a group at a theater in Chiang Mai this year. The beautiful dancers wore costumes in bright silks, woven with shiny gold and silver threads and decorated with jewels and pearls. Best of all, were the golden spired crowns, or *chada*. Mom says maybe someday I can go to the Dramatic Arts College in Bangkok where students train to be classical musicians and dancers. For now, I practice at home, dipping, gliding and swaying my arms to the slow rhythm of the music. I stretch my hands and fingers back just so.

Classical dance in Thailand started over 500 years ago in the royal court, but you can see it all over the country today. *Khon* dancing is the oldest and most famous style. It began as a way of telling the epic Ramakien. A classical *piphat* band (more on page 50) plays music, a chorus of singers tells the story, and the dancers act it out. It's really exciting. Hundreds of characters leap and twirl across the stage, acting out wild adventures and swinging their swords in great battles.

The khon was once performed only by men. That has changed but the steps and moves have stayed the same. The costumes are so amazing with gold and silver sparkling everywhere. And the coolest thing is the scary-looking masks worn by the monkeys, demons, hermits and other mythological characters in the story.

Characters from the Ramakien

Thai Khon Dance in Frankfurt, Germany

Lakorn nai classical dance (the kind I like best!) was first danced by women at the court. Most dancers today are still women, but there are some men too. Lakorn nai dance steps are very slow and graceful as dancers move to the music of a piphat band. They have glittery costumes like khon dancers, but they don't wear masks. These groups perform different kinds of stories like epic poems and love stories.

Lakorn nok is a less formal style of dancing, where the dancers wear simpler traditional clothes. Troupes of *lakorn nok* dancers travel to rural areas in Thailand and perform at temple fairs. These dancers tell folktales and stories about Buddha's life.

Another style of dance called *lakorn chatri* is popular in southern Thailand. These dancers mix *lakorn nok* steps with local folkdances.

Thai traditional dance

Folkdances

All over Thailand, traditional dances are performed at temple fairs, wedding celebrations, and festivals such the Buddhist holiday Vesak. My favorite local dance here in northern Thailand is one my grandmother taught me. It's called *Fon Sao Mai* or the silk weaving dance. We dance in a group with very slow, calm movements, a little like lakorn nai. The dance imitates different steps in the silk-weaving process.

Making Khon Masks

It takes over 100 hours to make one khon mask! The artists start with a clay model of the character's head and apply layer after layer of paper maché and sap from a lap tree. Then they paint the mask with different features and add glitter and gold. If it's a demon character, they add fangs made of pearl shells.

49

Traditional Thai Music

At school I'm learning to play the *khlui,* a bamboo flute. It's a perfect instrument for kids, because it only has a single reed to blow on and a few holes down the front that you cover with your fingers. Easy!

I also take lessons to learn how to play the *pi,* a double reed instrument like an oboe. It's a lot harder! My teacher is in a piphat orchestra (the name comes from the lead instrument, the pi) that includes oboes, flutes, drums, gongs and a xylophone. They play for khon and lakorn nai traditional dance performances, and also marionette and shadow puppet shows. Traditionally piphat musicians have been boys and men.

Tawan

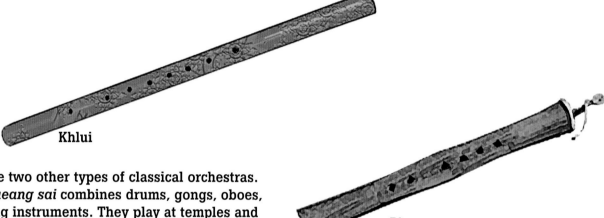

Khlui

Pi

There are two other types of classical orchestras. The *khrueang sai* combines drums, gongs, oboes, and string instruments. They play at temples and stick puppet shows.

The *mahori* orchestra first played in the royal court and consisted of women musicians. These groups have more string instruments, but no oboes. They often accompany singers.

Other Music

In Thailand we like all kinds of music. When we say "string" music (*phleng string*), it doesn't mean just *jakhis* and *saw samsais* or violins and cellos. "String" is the term for pop music in Thailand. Western pop and rock became popular in the 1960s (when my grandparents were young), and Thai bands began playing American and European music. In the 1990s Thai bands developed their own music based mostly on Western pop and rhythm and blues. Many of groups have English names and sing in both Thai and English. Like Western pop, Thai string is all about guitars, bass, keyboards, drums and vocals. The term string includes folk, indie, hip-hop, metal, country and any other types of popular music.

A number of Thai symphony orchestras play Western classical music as well as compositions from China and other Asian countries.

And if you like unique music, don't forget the Thai Elephant Orchestra, which Mari mentioned on page 17!

Here are some of the main instruments found in classical music groups along with the pi. Maybe you are learning to play an instrument that's similar to one of these.

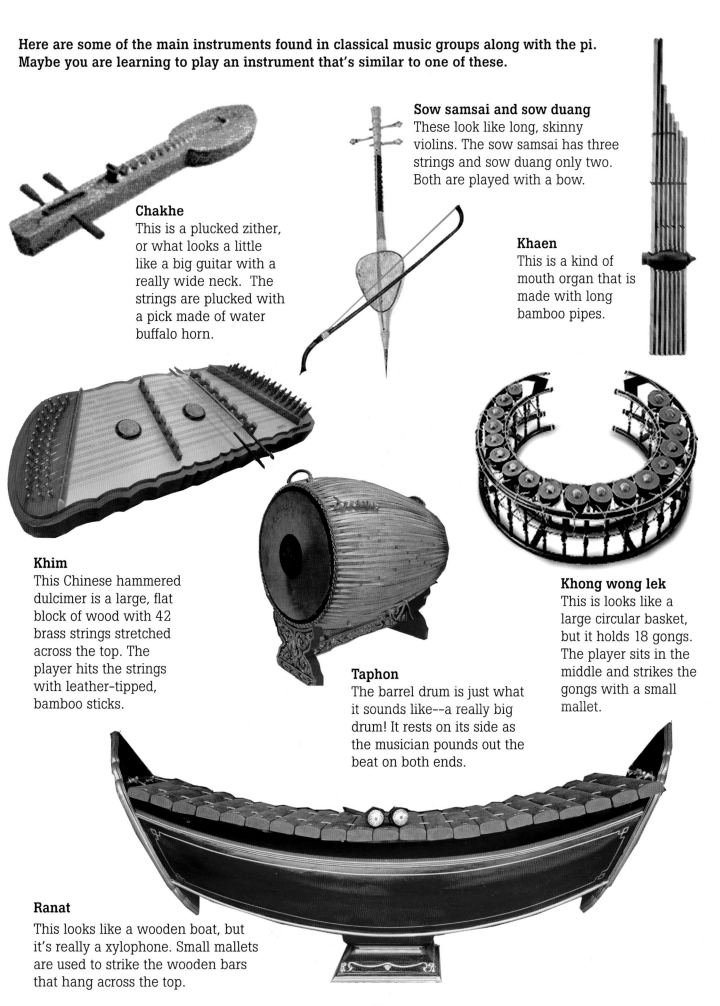

Chakhe
This is a plucked zither, or what looks a little like a big guitar with a really wide neck. The strings are plucked with a pick made of water buffalo horn.

Sow samsai and sow duang
These look like long, skinny violins. The sow samsai has three strings and sow duang only two. Both are played with a bow.

Khaen
This is a kind of mouth organ that is made with long bamboo pipes.

Khim
This Chinese hammered dulcimer is a large, flat block of wood with 42 brass strings stretched across the top. The player hits the strings with leather-tipped, bamboo sticks.

Taphon
The barrel drum is just what it sounds like--a really big drum! It rests on its side as the musician pounds out the beat on both ends.

Khong wong lek
This is looks like a large circular basket, but it holds 18 gongs. The player sits in the middle and strikes the gongs with a small mallet.

Ranat
This looks like a wooden boat, but it's really a xylophone. Small mallets are used to strike the wooden bars that hang across the top.

Make a Thai Shadow Puppet
And Perform Your Own Shadow Play!

Nang shadow puppet shows are a favorite with kids. Shadow figures bob across the stage, telling stories like the Ramakien and other tales of magic, adventure, and love. Traditionally puppets are made from cow or buffalo hide. In fact, Nang means hide. The puppets are held up against a white, see-through screen with bright lights behind them. The audience is on the other side of the screen so all they see are the puppets' shadows. The male puppets are always seen from the side, while female puppets face out toward the audience.

There are two types of shadow puppets in Thailand. *Nang Talung* puppet figures are about 19 inches (1.8 meters) tall and have an arm that moves. The puppeteers speak the lines or sing as they move their puppets about the screen.

Nang Yai puppets are figures set in a larger scene. They don't have moving arms and are much larger. Some are over 6 feet tall and can weigh up to 15 pounds (7 kilograms). You have to have strong arms to work with these puppets! Piphat bands play for the shows as the stories are told through singing, music and chanting.

A Nang Talung puppet of Sita, wife of Rama. (We call her Sida in the Ramakien.)

How to Make Your Own Shadow Puppet

Puppets are fun to make. Here's an easy one to try.

Supplies:

Template (explained below)
Heavy card stock (8½ by 11 inches/21.6 x 28 cm)
Scissors
Color markers or crayons

Glitter glue (optional)
Metal brad fasteners (for a Nang Tulang puppet)
Bamboo skewers or thin dowels
Clear tape

1. To start, you need a character. You can download all kinds of puppet templates online (just pop "shadow puppet templates" into your browser). Print it onto your card stock. Or, you could trace a favorite character from a book to make a template. Cut it out, place it on your card stock, and trace around it. You can also make up your own character and draw it onto your card stock.
2. Cut out your character.
3. Color and decorate the figures. If you are very careful, you can pierce the card stock with your scissors to cut out details that light can shine through. Ask your mom or dad to help.
4. Tape a bamboo skewer to the puppet's back. If your puppet needs two hands to operate, add another skewer.

You can hang up a white sheet and put a bright lamp behind it to show off your puppets. Have fun!

53

Traveling by Boat
Thailand is a Country With Hundreds of Waterways

One of my favorite ways to travel in Thailand is by boat.

Tawan

Last summer my family took a cruise boat up the Chao Phraya River from Bangkok to the ancient city of Ayutthaya. It was really fun to see the fields and towns along the way. And when we went to the beach in southern Thailand, I went fishing in a motor boat with my dad and brother. (I caught two fish!)

With over 100 rivers, lots of canals (called *klongs*), and oceans surrounding all of southern Thailand, boats are a big part of Thai life. They are used for travel, hauling goods, fishing, and just for fun! I love going with my mom in a motorized longboat called a *ruea hang* to the floating market (*Damnoen Saduak*) where farmers sell goods from their boats.

Sometimes on Saturdays my friends and I take the Skytrain to the Chao Phraya River and ride the ferry boat to the other end of the line in Bangkok. We see all kinds of boats: big barges, motorized long-tail boats, tourist boats, fishing boats, and row boats. Locals with shopping bags and tourists with cameras get on and off along the way.

The floating market is always fun!

On holidays the king or other members of the royal family float down the Chao Phraya River in one of the Royal Barges. But the big event is the Royal Barge Procession, which only happens every five years or so. This includes 52 golden royal barges. What a sight! If you miss it, you can visit the Royal Barge Museum in Bangkok to see a few of the best boats.

In September and October, when the water in the rivers runs highest, longboat (*ruea yao*) festivals are held on all the major rivers in Thailand. Kids love watching these races. The longboats, carved from a single log, are really long (100-160 feet or 30-50 meters) and narrow—two rowers can barely squeeze in next to each other. There are between 50 and 60 rowers per boat. Each boat represents a local Buddhist temple. It's pretty exciting to see them skim across the rivers, racing for the finish line!

The royal barge procession is a hundreds of years old tradition that happens only on very special occasions.

The most popular longboat competitions in Thailand are the Dragon Boat Races. The boats look like the longboat pictured on the left, but are carved at the prow (front end) and stern (back end) to look like dragons, like the Royal barge below. Dragon Boat Races originated in China more than 2000 years ago to honor the poet Qu Yuan who, it is said, cast himself into the river in sorrow over a Chinese government that had become corrupt. The races have become popular around the globe and follow a specific set of rules. The races in Thailand are some of the most exciting events of the year. Crews come from all over the world to compete.

Traditional Thai Clothing
Colorful Handwoven Thai Silk Textiles are Beautiful

On weekends and after school I wear shorts or jeans and a t-shirt. At school we wear uniforms—navy shorts with a white shirt. In rural villages like Mali's, girls and women often wear top and skirts made of cotton or hemp, and many boys and men wear cotton pants and collarless shirts. But for special occasions, like weddings, holidays, and festivals, we all dress up in our very best traditional clothes made of silk.

Boys wear long pants and a raj style, or Nehru jacket. Sometimes a checked or plaid sash, called a *pha khao ma*, is tied around the middle or worn over the shoulder.

Girls wear blouses and a long skirt called a *pha sin*, which has a special pattern across the bottom. For special occasions they may wear a shawl across their shoulder and front called a *pha sa bai*.

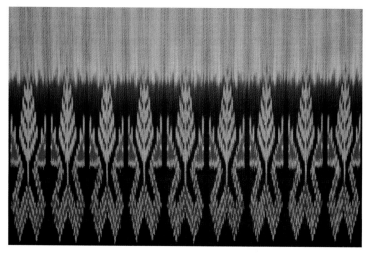

A sample of handwoven, handmade silk with natural dyes from Ban Tha Sawang, Surin Province, Thailand. Silk like this could be used to make a pha sin. Sometimes the pha sin's border is a separate piece that is sewn to the bottom of the skirt; other times, it's already woven into the fabric.

To Make a Phra Khao

Here's a phra khao that's easy to make. You can wear it to celebrate Loi Krathong or Songkran!

Supplies

White or light colored cloth
Iron and ironing board (Be sure you have your parents' permission and supervision when using these!)
Iron on seam tape. You can find this in any craft, fabric or general retail store.
Colored markers, fabric paint, and glitter glue
A ruler for drawing lines

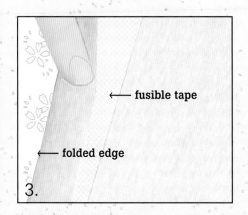

← fusible tape

← folded edge

3.

1. Measure around your waist.
2. Cut a piece of cloth 7 inches (18 centimeters) wide that is twice the length of your waist.
3. To hem your edges, fold an edge over about ¾ inches (about 2 centimeters) and slip a length of seam tape inside the fold. Press with the iron. Do this for all four edges. Make sure to make all four folds on the same side of the fabric. When you are finished hemming turn the fabric over.
4. Draw a checked or plaid pattern on the fabric with markers, fabric paint, or glitter glue. Add any other decoration you want.
5. Tie the sash around your waist or drape it over your shoulder, as Tawan is doing on page 56.

This pha sa bai and pha sin were part of an exhibit at the Bunka Fashion Institute in Tokyo, Japan. The pha sa bai is worn across the front and over the shoulder.

A pha khao ma is usually checked, often with stripes, like this one. Over the centuries, Thai men have used it as a belt, a scarf, a head wrap, a towel, a carrying cloth, a bathing suit and more.

Wild Animals — Big and Small
Thailand Has Incredible Animals, But Some Are Now Endangered

I n school, I've been learning about the thousands of wild animals—enormous, tiny, creepy crawling, swimming, flying—that live in Thailand. Some tigers, monkeys, and other animals are losing their homes as forests are cut down and towns continue to grow. But luckily, the government has set aside land for national parks, and private groups are working to protect the wildlife of Thailand, including my favorite, the elephants.

Here are some amazing animals on the top of my list to see. Have you heard of them?

Black and White Great Hornbill

This is a pretty funny looking bird. Its enormous, double yellow beak looks so heavy that I don't know how it can hold up its head. There are many different hornbills in Khao Sok National Park and other forests in southern Thailand. The Helmeted Hornbill looks more like a dinosaur than a bird!

Asian Palm Civit (also called a Toddy Cat)

These guys live in Doi Intanon National Park and other forests. But you'll have to come at night to see them. They live in the tree branches and sleep all day. They love to eat fruit!

Kitts Hog-Nosed Bat

Want to meet a bat the size of your thumb? This is the smallest mammal on earth. You'll have to visit the caves in Sai Yok National Park, because this is the only place in the whole world where they live!

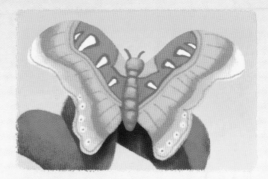

Atlas Moth

This is the largest moth in the world with wings that are over 10 inches across. The caterpillars spin cocoons that can be used to make silk, but it is harder to work with than silkworm cocoons.

Giant Catfish

Both these fish live in the Mekong River and are really BIG! They can be over six feet long—taller than most people in Thailand.

Muddskippers

This is another funny animal that looks like a cross between a fish and lizard. It is amphibious, so it lives in and out of the water. It is found on Phukhet island and other beach areas of southern Thailand. They actually skip across the water. That I've got to see!

We're so Proud to be Thai

One last thing I want to show you is the official flag of the Kingdom of Thailand and our national emblem. Our flag has stripes of red (for the land and people), white (for the Buddhist religion), and blue (for the king). What other countries do you know with these colors on their flags?

Tawan

The national symbol for the royal family and the Thai government is this really cool Garuda, the powerful king of birds. It's a mythological beast that is actually part bird and part man. And it's a god in both Hindu and Buddhist beliefs. Sometimes the Garuda looks a lot like an eagle and other times more like a really scary man with wings! You see the Garuda all over Thailand on flags, buildings, and at Buddhist and Hindu temples.

December 10 is Constitution Day. On this day in 1932 the first constitution was approved, making Thailand a constitutional monarchy. The royal family gives advice, but the prime minister and parliament run the government.

Khopkhun (thank you) for letting us show you around Thailand. I hope you liked learning about our life here. There are so many wonderful places to see and things to do. We hope you will come to visit Thailand soon!

Now that you've read our book, you can see why Thailand is called "The Land of Smiles." We enjoy life and have a lot of *sanuk* (do you remember what that means?). Maybe you can visit Thailand one day. Now that would be really *sanuk*! Don't forget to sing some songs, practice speaking Thai, play games, and eat some delicious Thai food. Make a shadow puppet or some yummy sate! Enjoy it all and come back soon!

La Kon — Goodbye

Author's Acknowledgments

I am very grateful to Warunee Prommanuwat, Thai Studies Teacher, at the NIST International School in Bangkok, Thailand, for sharing favorite Thai games, songs, and folktales, and answering my many questions. Thank you to Yuphaphann Hoonchamlong, Associate Professor of Thai, University of Hawaii at Manoa, for help in understanding the Thai language and transliteration of words in this book. I appreciate the help of Nonglug Waldorff, who teaches Thai at the Wat Sacramento Buddhavanaram for her assistance and for the recording on the book's webpage of the pronunciation of Thai words in the chapter "Speak Thai with Me." A special thanks to my family—my son Russell, who lived in Bangkok for two years, and my husband who helped me research materials in Thailand. I greatly appreciate the wonderful guidance of my editor, Terri Jadick and all the team at Tuttle. And finally, thank you to Patchuree Meesukhon and Vinit Yessman for their beautiful illustrations.

Books for Further Reading

Thai For Kids, Pictionary Vol. 1 by Naam Sanannok Sheakley, Illustrated by Nee Boonyarattaphan (South East Asian Language Publishers, LLC, Bristow, 2008)

The Life of Rice: From Seed to Supper by Richard Sobol (Candlewick Press, Somerville, Massachusetts, 2010)

Thai Tales: Folktales of Thailand Retold by Suparpom Vathanaprida (World Folklore Vol. 5, Libraries Unlimited, Westport, Connecticut, 1994)

The Breath of the Dragon by Gail Giles (Clarion Books, New York, New York, 1997)

The Girl Who Wore Too Much: A Folktale from Thailand by Margaret Read MacDonald with Suparpom Vathanaprida (August House, Atlanta, Georgia, Bilingual Edition 2015)

It Rains Fishes: Legends, Traditions and the Joys of Thai Cooking by Kasma Loha-Unchit (Pomegranate Communications, Portland, Oregon, 1995)

Websites

First Monkey Training School: http://www.firstmonkeyschool.com/

Thai Elephant Conservation Center: http://www.thailandelephant.org/en/index.html

Thai Elephant Orchestra: http://www.mulatta.org/thaieleorchpage.html

Surin Annual Elephant Roundup: http://www.earsasia.org/#!surin-roundup/c4u8

Sangkran New Year Water Festival: http://www.bangkok.com/information-festivals/songkran.htm#

Bangkok Sepak Takraw History: http://www.bangkok.com/sport-sepak-takraw/origins---history.htm#

Dragon Boat Festivals: http://www.dragonboatfestivalsthailand.com/

Boat Racing in Thailand (different types of boats and a good discussion on history of racing): http://www.thaiwaysmagazine.com/thai_article/2310_boat_racing_in_thailand/boat_racing_in_thailand.html

Thai National Parks: https://www.thainationalparks.com

National Geographic Kids—Thailand: http://kids.nationalgeographic.com/explore/countries/thailand

Index

ABOUT TUTTLE
"Books to Span the East and West"

Our core mission at Tuttle Publishing is to create books which bring people together one page at a time. Tuttle was founded in 1832 in the small New England town of Rutland, Vermont (USA). Our fundamental values remain as strong today as they were then—to publish best-in-class books informing the world about the countries and peoples of Asia. The world has become a smaller place today and Asia's economic influence has expanded, yet the need for meaningful information about this region has never been greater. Since 1948, Tuttle has been a leader in publishing books on the cultures of Asia. Our authors have won numerous awards and we have published thousands of titles on subjects ranging from martial arts to Asian crafts. We welcome you to explore the richness of Asia at www.tuttlepublishing.com.

Published by Tuttle Publishing, an imprint of Periplus Editions (HK) Ltd.

www.tuttlepublishing.com

Library of Congress Cataloging In Publication Data for this title is in progress.

ISBN 978-0-8048-4427-7

Distributed by

North America, Latin America & Europe
Tuttle Publishing
364 Innovation Drive
North Clarendon, VT 05759-9436 U.S.A.
Tel: (802) 773-8930
Fax: (802) 773-6993
info@tuttlepublishing.com
www.tuttlepublishing.com

Japan
Tuttle Publishing
Yaekari Building, 3rd Floor
5-4-12 Osaki, Shinagawa-ku
Tokyo 141 0032
Tel: (81) 3 5437-0171
Fax: (81) 3 5437-0755
sales@tuttle.co.jp
www.tuttle.co.jp

Asia Pacific
Berkeley Books Pte. Ltd.
61 Tai Seng Avenue #02-12
Singapore 534167
Tel: (65) 6280-1330
Fax: (65) 6280-6290
inquiries@periplus.com.sg
www.periplus.com

First edition
20 19 18 17 16   10 9 8 7 6 5 4 3 2 1   1607EP
Printed in Hong Kong

TUTTLE PUBLISHING® is a registered trademark of Tuttle Publishing, a division of Periplus Editions (HK) Ltd.

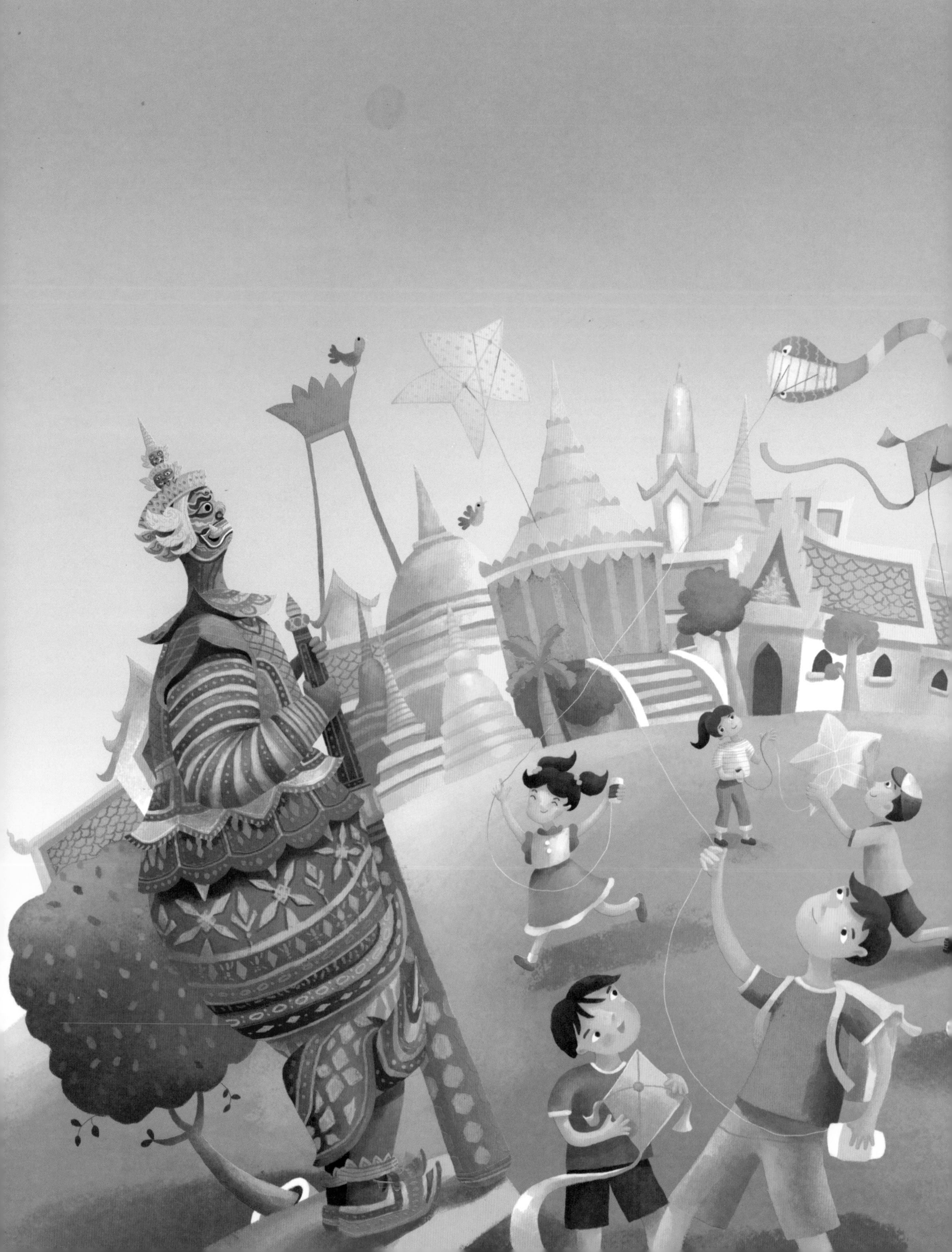